THE TESTIMONY OF THE TREES

typical phone-mast (cell tower) damage to tree, starting on the more irradiated side

THE TESTIMONY OF THE TREES

LYNNE WYCHERLEY

for Sarah,

Lynne Wycherley
x

Shoestring Press

Printed by imprintdigital
Upton Pyne, Exeter
www.digital.imprint.co.uk

Typesetting by narrator
www.narrator.me.uk
info@narrator.me.uk
033 022 300 39

Published by Shoestring Press
19 Devonshire Avenue, Beeston, Nottingham, NG9 1BS
(0115) 925 1827
www.shoestringpress.co.uk

First published 2018
© Copyright: Lynne Wycherley
© Cover design by Lynne Wycherley
© Photo of author by Jolyon Holroyd

The moral right of the author has been asserted.

ISBN 978-1-912524-19-8

ACKNOWLEDGEMENTS

Warmest acknowledgments to all
who have featured these poems:

Acumen, Artemis,
London Poetry Grip, New View
Poetry Scotland, Resurgence,
Tears in the Fence and
Temenos Academy Review,

also to *Agenda* and *Urthona*
for hosting 6-poem sequences
and to ES-UK health charity.

'Electrosensitive' appeared in the anthology
Songs for the Unsung (ed Joy Howard) Grey Hen 2017;
a version of 'Footprint' in *Her Wings of Glass*
(ed Myra Schneider et al) Second Light 2014;
'The Beekeeper, Buckfast Abbey' in
The Price of Gold (ibid.) Grey Hen 2011;
'Five Faces of the Severn' in *Speaking English:*
Poems for John Lucas (ed Andy Croft) Five Leaves 2007;
'Totems' in *Earth Songs: A Resurgence Anthology*
of Contemporary Eco-poetry (ed Peter Abbs),
Green Books, 2002

I dedicate this poetry
to the beauty at hidden risk from
polluting trends, especially breakneck
wireless expansion / addiction, and to
the courageous scientists, doctors and
others working for healing change
in the face of vast forces.

CONTENTS

The Testimony of the Trees

In 2016, scientists uncovered relentless damage
in trees much exposed to phone-masts' pulsing
microwaves (Germany), even at two miles:
"this constitutes a danger for trees worldwide"[1]
Added to the ever-growing science[2] that reveals
wireless risks to life, how it speaks to our times.

I am the tree on the skyline.
You alone
know my name.

I stand in prayer-reeds,
Paschal candles, fragrant.
Hold my flame.

~

I am Acer Rubrum, queen
of the reds,
leaves in flow

crimson to crimson, your
heart's 'now'.
Shall we dance?

AS IF A GALE

'Why fade the lotus on the water? Why fade
these children of the spring?'
– William Blake, *The Book of Thel*

We are floss, we are frail, in the ever-wind,
stems, serifs, pared back,

laterals lost to sky-wolves
as if a gale has shorn us from one side

staves to silence,
lamé to air, slow-motion.

In digital storms we are fraying

What finger picks at satin?
What shadow sits at the loom?

Leaves on the love-tree, fading

Hesitant child, where are you?
Your eyes wide to leaves, to wings.
Hózhó:"walking in beauty".

Who weighs the harm, silk-grams?
Comet assays: genetic strands.

Who weighs the heart?
Ma'at with her feather,
Thoth with his reed. All buried.

THE STRANGERS

'What we are doing to the forests... is but a mirror
reflection of what we are doing to ourselves'
– Mahatma Gandhi

Bleak, aloof,
they needled among us.
Grey lightning-streaks through the living.

Phone-masts, cell-towers, WiMax.
Verticals, a cold-edged gleam.

Marching steel-steel-steel

Cadres on rooftops,
microwaves pulsing through stucco,
bone: nano-hailstones.

The strangers. Ghosts to feed
the screen-addicted ghosts.

Marching steel

We are hallowmas-in-summer,
rust-tinged leaves

strange, someone says, *there's been
no drought*, hands mid-text,
eyes in data-fix

while daylight dips half-seen
trailing saris, Indian dyes

in gloriam Dei.

TROUBLED LIGHT

'The call of the garden will not be readily silenced'
– Jeremy Naydler, philosopher

Leaves fail. Needles fall.
The fir-tree stands in her tannins,
small fireworks gone to ash.

Trailing our tresses, our
troubled light

or swept at height,
a lean hand reaching for heaven.

Nitrosative, no caress.
Life-made-oxide: rusting dress.

No sea-mark in data storms.
A birch in sail: moon-rigged,
a chestnut: brigantine.

Unseen our bowlines loosen
on one side. Lateen to mizzen,
sternpost to stemson.

Where are the almoners,
the scroll-artists,
Rinceaux borders
in a Book of Hours, their
fine lines drawn through must?

Slow attrition, day-night-day.
Finite, life-line: DNA.

AMULET

'A kid's brain on tech looks like a brain on drugs'[3]
– Dr Nicholas Kardaras, clinical professor of addiction

She's just looked up—
a candid gaze, shell-like face,

lunette. Her *Silent Spring*
an opal under fire: amulet.

Her then: our now,
how the roulette spins—

adverts! adverts!—
'set phasers to stun'

> *click-rates—war-games—*
> *children in screens*
> *their neurons firing, firing*

while the slow wonder
of a primrose waits

its silk word held to heaven.

> *My inch of sky, fathomless*
> *my well, my vowel*
> *my peace.*

TARANTELLA

'The human body is an electro-chemical instrument
 of exquisite sensitivity'
 – G J Hyland, biophysicist, Nobel nominee

*Now Vathi's mountain-birds have gone
and the barren rod is king.*

What thins the garden?
Whispers in muslin,
 not sieverts but a hidden pulse.
The tadpoles feel it, the sparrows
mortal damage; fewer nests.
Follicles; your cells.
The foetus in her velvet hall
and cell-phones held too close.

*When did heart-rates quicken,
a stop-valve hover, stall?
The digital dance spin
out of control? Tarantella.*

For every tree: a spike.
For every child: two more.
The tested bees grew shrill.
Routers, boosters, leeched to walls—
chips in dermis, clothing, pills—
how the virus burrows,
how the sand-storm drills.

*Where is the treehouse, the den?
The 'last child in the woods'?
Living aerial: played-out eyes.
Love, my love, return to me.*

EPIPHANIES

'Every sparkle…will remain vividly perceptible'
– Rudolf Steiner: on leaves seen spiritually

Out of the dawn, the mist, we are
Japanese prints on sky-silk

red-pepper stamens
pink-tinted snow
lux beatisima.

> *Sunlight in leaves:*
> *bel canto. Where are the breves,*
> *the antiphons, as*
> *human souls sing back?*

Delicate, how the balance tips—
digital tools, *panchiko* balls
sold as fun—commodity-run—
live less, post more!
phones' event horizons,
time falling in
^l8r? l8r (hookup later? later)

where the Virtual skims
the sun, the moon:
shadow peddling shadows.

> *Iodine in our branches*
> *astringent stars, Orion's spurs—*
> *hunter call the cub*
> *to heel: Fenrir.*

THE MIRROR-HOUSE

'To protect our children, ourselves, and our
ecosystems, we must reduce exposure'
– Professor Martin Blank: announcing the 240-scientist appeal to
the U.N.[4]

What warps the weft?
Microwaves sold as 'safe' and yet—
Sperm-tails vanish.
Minnows slip the brain's fine net.
Genetic threads: undone.

What warps the weft
so subtly? The white tree
of nerves, red tree of blood
and warning science unsung.

> *Sachiko, child-of-happiness,*
> *where are you? Umeka*
> *child-of-plum-blossom, Naoki*
> *the boy-tree. Flavines, fragrant.*
> *Bark's ripple: an infinite river.*

Selfies: humanity in a mirror-house
404: lost in device, S4L: spam for life
husked in pixels, URLs, a second skin.

Not a child but an *end user.*
Not a carer but a *high-speed interface.*
Not eyes but an *emoticon*

and the river's tears
running.

THE FIRE JUGGLERS

'I watched the number of autistic kids skyrocket'
– Professor Martha Herbert

> *Touch-screens, weevil-bloom.*
> *Channels, channels, consumers consumed.*

Here come the corporate fire-jugglers.
Bored with tobacco? Beat this!
Microwaves, millimetre waves.
Delicate risks to body, skin.
Not content with 1 in 3 cancer?
Boost your chances
with the latest upgrade!

24:7, a toxic tisane,
smart-homes drilled by smart-chips,
smart-meters. *All-wireless, hurry!*
Strip away the vines,
the safe connections: fibre to screen.
Strip away clematis,
honeysuckle, clean.

> *Electro-blight. Creeping headaches,*
> *hollow nights; Jenny Fry.*

Bury the warnings; spike the sky.
Hurry! Make way.
Expunge the 'not-spots',
the oases. Eden-dots

sanctum sanctorum.
World-smoke.

PEREGRINE FALCON

'I have journeyed among the dead forms...
pillar to pylon...but A a a domine Deus'
– David Jones

A star-pin on midnight's sleeve,
what might a seraph,
pellucid, see—

addiction: radiation
addiction: radiation
money-spin.

Look up: higher than the woods,
the Wellgate. Higher than corbels,
the 'Bishop's Eye', its
whorl of glass, wry noon.

A finial, slate-blue.
Ink pupils in daffodil rings
where Lincoln spins, spins.
  Spirit—peregrine—what can
  you see? Bark under stress?
  Fricative breath, skylines
  hung from antennas?
Sky-wrapped. Its coverts
sleek, swept back.
  Where is a lull, a pause?
  A clause for wisdom,
  a vase for new light?

Trees in prayer: as if its spear
could part the blue.
Run greed through. Striking
the '*dead forms*' dead.

SEESAW

'Cell-phones, tablets, wifi etc…are damaging the
living cells in our bodies'
– Professor Martin Blank, DNA researcher

I am the ash in the wind-grass.
Hear how the lark unlatches
the blue: sings diamonds.

Ci-ça, ci-ça, online–offline
the tilting-board of tongues
byte-packet / song-thrush
biometric / empathy
radiation / awen.

Ci-ça, ci-ça, online–offline
myPad, Wi, profit machines,
pulsed microwaves dressed
in ribbons *mi-Ted, Pii*—
no warnings.

A blackbird sings: the boy
looks up—a seesaw
tilting from screen to sky
I'm jet-stone, dulcet,
jack-of-the-twigs—
my orange bill sings the sun!

his face open—celandine—
a chink in time. Closing?

I am the pine by the mountain stream.
If life could lift, spines uncurl
in lit water: soul-ferns.

FIRSTBORN

'Sirius singing in the branches of the ash,
the world large again'
– Edmund Cusick (1962–2007)

White-haired in moonlight, our shapes
struck from rock to stars
we are the firstborn, the elders,
our sugar-paper leaves: your lungs.
Pores, lenticels, breathing;
oxygen at night, a seamless exchange.

We cradle stars, infinities,
weightlessly carry their snow,
the world-wheel turning in charcoal.

> *Tousled head, sleep on,*
> *sky-coloured eggs,*
> *the oak-bug in her taffeta,*
> *moth pupa in fibreglass.*

> *Sleep, sleep, in the world's wood.*
> *Vibirnum lantana: moon-scent.*
> *Sorbus aria: lullaby.*

Forest-deep, we'd
shield you, durmast and bole,
but still you drive deeper,
gigabytes: an alien god, 5G
and children schooled in worship
still awake. Cheekbones

lit with eerie light.
Crinoids in shape-shifting seas.

A PRAYER ACROSS TIME

'Workers in a Swedish office block have been
implanted with microchips'
— *The Times*

Love, do not sleep: it is coming;
do not sleep: meet needle
with needle, heald-frame, leaf.

Where do you live? Rail-sped
as copses, brakes, rush by—
a train: the-shell-of-a-train
a phone: the-shell-of-a-phone.
Box in box, estrangement squared,
the apple's scented integer mislaid
calling at: 4G, 5G
smoked-out cities.

Where do you live: a data lens?
Third eyelid, bat-wing.
How grey the veil, how thin.
Oak, beech, our branches inked
on alizarin. Michaelmas fire,
a hare in flight, unseen.

Where is your friend? Dizzy, spent:
he's fled the hornet-nest,
the lightning, DNA in
a jewel-pouch for safe-keeping.
Lost friends, lost names—
prayers across time—
birds of paradise
in Faraday cages
fled from the fleeing world.

BAMBERG: A MAPLE SPEAKS

'How with this rage shall beauty hold a plea
Whose action is no stronger than a flower?'
– Shakespeare, Sonnet 65

Forget-me-nots,
blue mist, bathe me.
I pray for a kinder sky
that never comes.

No shelter from Altenburg, castle of masts,
the red rake of Franconia.

A woman steps from her taser-house,
tablet in hand.

What thieves me thieves her too,
slow-mo
Zeitlupe
larghissimo.

No shelter in the old eaves,
Hegel's flight from la Grande Armée,

Pedestrians trade blizzards.
I shrink: they grow.
'Bas-de-page'
I wait for the axe.

I was a word made beauty.
Now I am nil, winter's nail.

Know me.

ELECTRO-FAUST

'Man conquered the Black Death but he has created
new problems: electromagnetic-field pollution'
– Professor Yury Grigoriev

Cross-fade, digital noise
0 1, 0 1: needle-eyes.

Trace it: a branch in cobalt
where metal spores oust stars:
strange crustaceans, drones.

No 'white zone' in future-sleet,
subtle, the lace of life
left bare.

Yukiko, 'snowdrop-child',
where are you?
Eden-dot, light's dew.
Lending your wick, your dazzle.

No 'white zone'. Electro-Faust
in space, on land,
micro-wands: antennas.
No 'white zone': will a genome
furl its ladder

leave love midair

Dante's light receding
in pale rungs?

VIGIL (I)

'[5G] would irradiate everyone, including the most
vulnerable to harm'
– Dr Ron Powell, physicist

I am the gold
in your night-glass,
vision; genome; meme.
Eden of dream.

Candles. Up-draft. Love flies
to the raven-loft,
a lit straw in her bill.

Candles, voices, rising.
Chaff in the wind, *sing with us.*
> *Heal homes, heal skies,*
> *curb SARS, save lives,*
> *clean connectivity: VLC,*
> *fibre-to-fibre, progressive.*
Tongues, trees, *sing with us.*

Polyphonies, professors:
Belpomme, Lai, Hardell—
brave refrains, kites of the sun
science suppressed (Hecht)
cancers and masts (Dode)
your brain's pelisse (Salford)
Pall: *the key,* Johansson …

If notes could shield, if nests
'*la flèche ne passera pas*'—
Love flies to the raven-loft,
a lit straw in her bill.

VIGIL (II)

'the soul said, Is this what you think it means
to be human?'
– C G Jung

> *Lost again: the sloe's*
> *horizon. A raison-gift,*
> *the black Isis, her sine-curves*
> *wooded, pungent.*

> *Lost to perception: her*
> *loess and fen. Lost to the barrens*
> *DAS, iDEN. Who will*
> *befriend their own soil?*

Life / not-life, an eerie dance
WYRN? ('what's your real name?')
L09, RU18? clasping the ice
too close, your
living hair: 'her' glass

and then—
how it fanned the news,
a cold ripple through world-blue:
the couple who reared
a virtual 'child' while
their infant starved: died.[5]

> *Hold her, hold her*
> *whoever you are, her*
> *sting in the heart—*
> *the heart must not die—*
> *the sting must live*
> *seed; quickbead; orchid.*

LYCHGATE

'A data exchange between algorithms is not a
living exchange, not communion'
– Rowan Williams

Out of the dearth, the drought
adware, spyware, the
synapse-taken-hostage freed to air—

> *lung-fish evolve again*
> *sip breeze, taste sky*

> *sand-lizard shed your digital skin,*
> *zeroes, scales; blink again*

> *on the russet rock where*
> *the outback basks, dreams;*

> *tree-geckos sing, life-layers,*
> *arpeggio in the roof-palms.*

Out of the dearth, the drought
IP addresses, IoT
electrical pins in micro-wings,
'connections' spun from smog.

Out of the drought,
needing a new Silk Road
or a pilgrim-thread to paradise

> *feet on the soil, deer-shy,*
> *the silt sensual—strange—*

> *a rain-fly's nest: a stupa*
> *a pollen-trace: a puja.*

WATER-BEADS

'I think all who are…working on this, going
against the current, we have the souls of poets'
– Dr Alfonso Balmori, biologist

So near—so far—
where is the tree on the threshold
where beauty hangs its star?

Where smalt runs clear
from 'smart' to wise
blithe river of air
not pixels but bees

where DNA twins safely,
damselflies, bleu-céleste,
each skelf a tiny heaven.

So near—so far—

Where *Tara* steps from
a water-bead: a star.

So near—

Where rose windows
speak their peace
pluperfect in a stone garden

the had been, the yet to be
serenitas nobis Domine.

'THE LULLINGSTONE OAKS'

'Nor must be forgot…the translucent amber'
– Samuel Palmer, 1828

Indian ink, heft in the shine—
how the oaks take life
in his cinnamon eyes
'barky furrows…these lords of the forrest'

> *Far, how you ebbed from us,*
> *cold-beyond-cold. Kevlar,*
> reductio, *deserts of code.*

> *Space-walkers, stumbling;*
> *driverless tractors, driverless cars,*
> *hung from the not-here, frying.*

> *If birds could laugh! could cry,*
> *jays—magpies—blue-jade.*

Almost translucent, the light
winning through: *citrinatis*
on white gouache

> *Cinders, strays: how you return,*
> *as if our stillness moves you,*
> *heartwood soothes you*

as lanterns quicken—
seeds from his soul—
stooks; apples; *rubedo*, whole.

THE EYES OF A FOX

'One tree…opens the flower of the world,
infinite'
– Kathleen Raine

A taper—a tine—I am
cedar-made-breeze: breathe me.
A five-fathom shiver, quench
of deep green: life-scent.

Sapphires in time, the light
of her mind: Mary Webb.
No glass can hold her
fully, no screen

as she stands—wild in the wild,
a child of the Wrekin
'now the four winds
stand up to sing…'

shutters flung wide
to earth-meets-sky, the rowan.
Her fox in her arms,
topaz and wine, the jolt

of its eyes—a mirror's
surprise—your
rawness: exquisite.

AT THE YEAR'S NOON

'In the center grew one mighty flowering tree
to shelter all the children'
– Black Elk

The sapling said: bro,
where' you been?
This Is Summer

He's lithe, a flame,
no house can hold him—
Richard Jefferies—he'll walk
for miles! Alive to the alive,
screen-free, *'the leaves…*
as if I could feel all
the glowing life'

inviting you with him
'the soul…finds freedom
in the sun and sky'
the downlands' pour, hatching
doors to summer
in your heart

a leaf: a sutra
a horizon: a psalter

where the breeze jay-walks,
jinks, in your hair—
where buildings

part to soil-skin, planet-rim

lifting you—
on its wing.

BREATHING SPACE

'As doctors we have addressed the chemical but
 not the electromagnetic'
– Dr Andrew Tresidder, GP

> *Screens that read you,*
> *cameras to 'feed' you—*
> *how infrared eye-trackers*
> *meter your gaze,*
> *how microwave sensors*
> *inveigle their 'eyes'—*
> *your space or theirs?*
> *who let them crowd in?[6]*

To curb radiation,
to rinse a room

a Waldorf school
a Taoist broom

a glade, a pool
moss-agate, a jewel

gwyrdd, awel
a breath blowing through

where imagination
steps forward

Puck, from his exile,
Wodwo, in green

mute—eloquent—
a leaf for a tongue.

WILD DIAMONDS

'Those who dwell among the beauties and mysteries
 of the earth are never alone'
 – Rachel Carson

A leaf, fractal,
at your window, a lisp
of dawn in your sleep—

come to the russets,
the whin-field. Leveret heart
how you leap!

To walk
into the real—the Real—
social; sensual; sacral

where finches gust,
live atoms—
gorse-scent, saffron—

five-petal rays, blackthorn's
'Glad Day'. The dazzling

embrace of the sun.

Sun in our leaves,
sun in the rain:
wild diamonds.

To face
the sky: no in-between.
Its harebell note of heaven

your breath re-homed, your
marrow, bones, your
heartbeat in
the Eden of its haem

as first drops fall,
quantum percussion, each
cyan-pearl a minim

on your skin.

> *Our leaves, seeds,*
> *re-selved in the rain,*
> *sun-in-the-rain*
>
> *diamonds, wholes,*
> *infinitesimals*
>
> *re-homing you*
> *in beauty.*

NOTES ON THE SEQUENCE

1 'Radiofrequency radiation damages trees…' Waldmann-Selsam et al, Science of the Total Environment 1;572, 2016. (For risks to residents notice, for example, the charity EM Radiation Research Trust, UK, and Dode 2011, Gandhi 2014, R-Ortega 2016, Zothansiama 2017).

2 e.g. i) International EMF Scientist Appeal to the UN and WHO (240 scientists, authors of over 2,000 papers in the field) urging safety reforms, education, child protection, more use of fibre instead of wireless, etc. ii) bioinitiative.org iii) Wycherley, *theecologist.org*

3 Dr Kardaras is author of *Glow Kids* 2016

4 *See note 2*

5 BBC/New York Times 5.3.2010

6 invasive trend to track your pupil size etc., whilst online, for marketing purposes

---

p. 4 – *Hózhó*: Navajo philosophy. *Comet assays*: reveal DNA strand breaks from output from 3G devices etc. (see e.g. REFLEX project).

p. 5 – *Pulsing microwaves*: increasingly shown to affect life, this 'radiofrequency' radiation is transmitted by mobile-phone masts (cell towers), WiFi antennas, cordless-phone stands (nonstop: for risks see Fragapoulou/Alasdair Philips), tablets unless in flight mode (notice the Powerwatch article on Lerchl 2015), smart-meters (harsh spikes: Drs David Carpenter / Martin Pall) and so on; even Bluetooth can harm living cells (Margiritis 2013).

p. 6 – *Jeremy Naydler*. *Gardening as a Sacred Art*. He also notes '*technological developments are not taking place in an ideological vacuum, but within a highly materialistic philosophical matrix*' New View autumn 2012. *Oxide*: free radical or genetic damage are the most common toxic findings from wireless exposure, including near-field WiFi damage to animals' organs (tinyurl.com/wifi40). *Rinceaux* (abbey): leafy manuscript borders.

p. 7 – *Rachel Carson*: *Silent Spring* was strafed by industry. Her words resonate today—'*the public… is fed little tranquilizer pills of half truth*'.

p. 8 – *Vathi*, Samos: vertiginous bird losses since phone masts (cell towers) installed. Ditto around Mount Nardi—see *ehtrust.org*.

Tadpoles: 90% mortality 100m from phone-masts, Balmori 2010. *Sparrows*: Spanish, Belgian, Indian research. *Foetus*: risks of ADHD, Divan 2008; Aldad 2012. *Bees*: mobile-phone signals provoked the shrill sound that cues abandoning hives, Favre 2011. *Sachiko* etc., Japanese first names. '*Last Child in the Woods*': Richard Louv 2005 and eponymous movement for childhood access to nature, USA.

p. 9 – *Rudolf Steiner*: cautioned against blind use of electromagnetism. *Panchiko*: addictive game with steel balls, Japan. *L8R*: 'later' (texting slang). *Fenrir*: (mythical wolf) swallowed the sun during Ragnarök.

p. 10 – *Brain's net*: risks to our blood-brain barrier (protects the brain from toxins) including from passive exposure to devices (Salford), supported by recent Chinese research. *Nerves/blood*: risks related to autism, for example, and oxidative harm to our immune cells.

p. 11 – *Jenny Fry*: pupil badly affected by school wireless radiation; she tragically took her own life in 2016 (*see Belpomme 2015*: nearly 700 patients with disabling symptoms from wireless exposure had poor brain blood-flow and toxic markers; where retested, this improved with wireless avoidance). *Desperately Seeking White-zone*, the beautiful film by Marc Khanne, charts the rise in affected people.

p. 14 – *5G*: poised to ramp up microwave pollution (especially millimetre waves) using dense transmitters—please see *ehtrust.org* and mounting international condemnation, including the Appeal by scientists and doctors for an EU moratorium: *5Gappeal.eu*.

p. 15 – *Data lens*: data-streaming contact lenses. *Faraday cage*: microwave-blocking canopies used for symptom relief, including, for example, by physicist Dr James McCaughan.

p. 17 – *Yury Grigoriev*: venerable chair of Russia's non-ionising radiation protection body, regarded as a 'grandfather' of this field. *Metal spores*: 'space race' to launch tens of thousands of internet satellites (with grave eco-risks—see 5G links above); notice 'radiofrequency' radiation can harm leaves, Haggerty 2010. *White-zone*: area free of RF-EMF pollution (such as 4G, 5G).

p. 18 – *SARS*: radiation rating for mobile phones/tablets. *VLC*: pending bio-tests, a way to enjoy digital gifts using light. *Fibre-to-*

fibre (e.g. cable internet to screens): safest option, often carbon-saving—see Re-inventing Wires (Dr T Schoechle) / Katie Singer. *Professors*: to name only a few of the many inspiring, cautioning scientists: Dominique Belpomme, Henry Lai, Lennart Hardell, Karl Hecht, Adilza Dode, Leif Salford, Martin Pall, Olle Johansson. *Key*: Professor Pall's mechanism of wireless harm; this gift to humanity won a Global Medical Discovery listing, supporting calls for safer technologies, especially in schools/hospitals. *la flèche ne passera pas*: 'the arrow will not get through'—French Resistance code.

p. 19 – *Jung*: the global dive into risky, disembodied wireless trends reminds me of his words *'the spirit of the depths said to me: look into your depths, pray to your depths, waken'* plus Dr Iain McGilchrist on left-brain hegemony *'The world as a whole would become virtualized… on its own it is like a zombie, a sleepwalker'*. *DAS*: small masts. *L09*: 'life online'.

p. 20 – *Rowan Williams*: (former Archbishop of Canterbury) addressing Resurgence's 50th anniversary symposium, Oxford 2016. *IoT*: internet of things, producing smog from countless 'connected' objects, adding to an emerging sick-building syndrome.

p. 21 – *Tara*: 'star', dear to Buddhists.

p. 22 – *Lullingstone Oaks*: Samuel Palmer (painting) 1828. *Kevlar*: bullet-proof metal for satellites/troops. *Driverless tractors*: set to ramp up RF pollution. *VR*: virtual or 'augmented' reality, often using wireless headsets. *Citrinitas/Rubedo*: alchemy's late stages.

p. 23 – *Fox*: Mary Webb's totem in her novel *Gone to Earth*.

p. 24 – Quoting Richard Jefferies' *The Life of the Fields* and *Nature Near London* 1883–4.

p. 25 – *Dr Andrew Tresidder, GP*: a trustee of charity Electrosensitivity UK for people ill with wireless/EMF exposure symptoms; see inspiring online talks by colleague Dr Erica Mallery-Blythe, also Brian Stein CBE. *Waldorf schools*: (Steiner-inspired) nurture time in nature and tactile skills. *gwyrdd, awel*: green, breeze (Welsh).

p. 26 – *'Glad Day'*: or 'Dance of Albion', William Blake (art) 1794.

Coda: a gift, a grace

MAGNOLIA STELLATA

Bring me again
to the breathing garden
insects singing
in scented air
as buds quicken

lilac and viburnum,
wave cambering
over lit wave
to a taller, white
intensity—

hints of Kailash
or the Hindu Kush,
a not-quite-snow
or flame—
and I sit

on the rim of heaven.
Life-made-vision.
Hostage to
a hatchery
of stars.

FOOTPRINT

Hover-bee in crab-apple
painting dust in scented caves,
you give more than you take

while we burn more
than continents can bear:
our deficit grows daily.

Cell-towers, fracking wells,
stripping the sea. Earth's
magic apple grows hollow.

Let appetite be local, blithe,
field-paths survive,
the pressure of my being

no more than this—
the kiss of a leaf,
a solute in light.

THE SILENT HEADLAND

Orkney

Who stole the living silver from the sea?
Motes in the air, balletic?
The snap of fans, sunlit vanes.
Terns in their thousands, gone.

In this place that has no swallows
they'd arrive like a gift, a grace.
Miraculous spirits
from visions of snow,
Antarctic summers
under their wings, blinding.

I close my eyes: how they'd
dart and swirl, a solar ghost
that swept in dazzling atoms.

Now the sand-eels that feed them
are lost to the north,
the sea's warmed drift,
life's substrata hustled away
plankton tectonics.

Who stole the living silver from the sea?
Motes in the air, balletic?
Corporate oil.
Corporate coal.
And you, dear friend. And me.

ON MIDSUMMER HILL

for Ian

The sunset holds us,
love's long moment.
Bronze in cobalt. Candescent, calm.

The sun drifts down
like an angel from Chagall,
our world still burning in its arms.

ADONIS BLUE

Here on the common we're closer to sky,
    higher than the roofs in the valley
that roost, huddled, with umber wings.
    This raffia page, fee-free, where
coxcomb, fatches, stitch their flames.

Beryline, a blink in the grass.
    Here—there—a hinge of light.
Just how a moment can bare its grace,
    a smile's new moon, stranger's face.
Adonis: I know you; sky-shred,
    I know you. Itinerant word. Elusive
spirit in a shrink-wrapped world.

Fragment of heaven find me. Brief,
    forever, un-blind me. From alchemies
of hope and pain; the piquant sun,
    emollient rain. Out of the common
and its breezy mane: come.

POACHER'S CHILD

i.m. my father

I'm your silt-shod daughter,
the moon in my hair
as if Her silver is safe there,
as if the elusive could live in my heart.

"You'd make a good poacher" you said,
brows raised, as I skirted gravel
like satin. Serious praise—
a gauging look in your hazel eyes
because you are my daughter, after all.

Weighed, weightless, in your gaze,
how a child could be carried
in a weave of light, cradle
of reeds; your smoker's wheeze.

Now I tread deftly through summer's leaze,
raindrops on water, not wanting
to put trout to flight,
the partridge in her tickle-grass,
hares inked in orpiment.

Finding a way to you, back through
thorn-brakes, famished years,
your rustling laugh

and filched from those who'd thieve us—
overlords, offshore funds—
a pheasant's sheen
still warm.

ELECTRO-SENSITIVE

They could be you:
your sawdust fatigue,
your headache's red axe.
Dizziness, tinnitus,
your sleep elusive
as a turquoise moon.

They could be you:
exiled from rooms.
Pub, office, café, train.
Lit glades where friends
would gather, lost amber.
Their lives shrink

as routers grow,
microwaves that drill, drill,
no warnings—tablets,
smartphones, cordless—
vipers, hornets,
smart-meter needles.

They could be you:
phosphors, pearls
dashed aside for data-speed.
As profits pour. Adverts roar.
Wireless! Wireless!
Corporate greed.

FIVE FACES OF THE SEVERN

for Ivor Gurney

Hock Cliff, the Severn's hook. I face
barbed wire and mud. No dysentery
though dark thoughts
                    breed here. I trace
wool on the wire, a snared sky.

Grey-green, mid-tide, it slides at my feet,
too calm to mirror you, sedate
but the sun
               conjures a scarlet hat
and all the fires of Framilode are lit.

Night-walker: you'd take this path between
water and moon, bit-work or none.
Free, half-fed,
                your thoughts in spate—
the river spreads its thinning light.

A ghost in the east, Stone House.
No chance of a 'blighty' to send you home.
Electricity
             ousts the sun. Across
your page the obstinate Severn runs.

Do you remember elver-fishermen
setting their lamps by the shore, red stars?
Now they've gone
                you move in
supple clauses, slip through our fingers.

SKYLINE WITH FOX

She crests the rim—

a living flame,
her lantern poised in a dream-field
smoking with alders.

She barks in the night—

slips a blade
between soil and sky,
the drift-nets of my sleep.

She's rust on the run—

woodland percussion.
She's in my pulse,
the castanets of my blood.

———

Today the fields have shrunk
through cold glass.

I scan for her broach,
a copper clasp

life's red ink
in the harried grass.

THE BEE-KEEPER, BUCKFAST ABBEY

in memory

Each day he takes the veil,
walks to a wedding. Brother Adam
keeper of bees, his first years
stung with torments, a dab
of salt and onion juice for stings.

Age twelve, how he trembled
when the first swarm rose
and sang. Freed from a skep,
it busied its seeds on burlap,
suspended its storm from a tree.

Now his hands glide, practised
as a lover, on the crowded
lattice, the river of bees.
Gentled to peace, a thrum
of intercession in their wings.

Their atoms fizz; sun-gatherers,
they scent the wick his litanies
will rise on. With heather,
dogwood, red clover,
transubstantiations of summer.

He stoops to the queen. Sunk
in her tracery, brooding her dream.
Our Lady. At night the brothers
pace their bounded rooms.
She beds in gold, her tomb.

Apis mellifera: even the name
speaks honey, easing the iron
of the Rule. Soft wax, sweet wine.
He lifts a comb: his dark eyes
read its amber light and shine.

TOTEMS

As if retrieving pebbles
        filmed with shine
from the curved spine of a beach,
        waves lisping
our faces stung with salt, our
        talk fresh with
discovery, we carried
        each season
to our door; catkins, frost-flakes
        of blossom,
the flotsam of our journeys,
        sweet chestnuts'
porcupines, pectorals of
        cones. Turning
varied textures in our hands,
        fleetingly
touched by their strangeness, subtly
        changed. Bringing
the outside in, so the house
        swam in its
wider rhythms, the flow of
        storm-clouds, hills,
moraine; the shuttling arc
        of the sun.

WAITING FOR THE STARS

I wait for you at the workday's end,
whispers in cerulean.
Dusk inks the downs,
the valley. Cars swerve home;
a chain of rooms log-on.

Whispers, vespers, light-on-the-wing—
sleet deeper than
our data-feeds and drones,
their nano-stealth
in the needled night

where a window-child
is restive, peeled from glare;
where L.E.D.s
dishevel owls, their
soft notes hustled from the woods.

Star-sleet soothe
our fast-lane lives, screen-shot eyes.
Speak to our sparks,
our red-shift hearts
though data runs them through.

I wait for ice-points to
crisp in the blue—
lit words in the rushing darkness.